WE THE PEOPLE NEVER WERE

How America Designed Power
And Sold Us the Illusion of Democracy

Renee Moore

At first, I could only name the feeling.
Then I realized the problem wasn't me.
The math wasn't mathing.
Ain't This Some Fucked Up Shit!
We The People Decide

— Early working title

Letter from the Author

I was born into this country and raised to love it. Not critically.

Not conditionally. Just love it—no questions asked.

I was taught the stories early: the bravery, the freedom, the promise. I was taught that if I worked hard, followed the rules, and believed, I too could achieve the American Dream. And for a long time, I tried to believe that the gap between the story and lived experience was my own error. Like I missed a step. Like, I didn't hustle hard enough. Like I wasn't patient enough.

I was wrong. It wasn't me.

The American Dream was just another marketing slogan, used to sell a false illusion. Patriotism is supposed to feel grounding. For many Americans, it feels confusing. We are told we live in the greatest democracy on Earth while watching our needs debated like inconveniences. We are told our voices matter, even as decisions are made far beyond our reach. We are told to trust institutions that rarely show up when trust is tested.

This book exists because I'm done believing, waiting, and wishing things will somehow work out or change for the better. I'm done with the quiet dissonance—devotion without protection, loyalty without reciprocity, sacrifice without acknowledgment. We are asked to love a country that increasingly treats its citizens as placeholders rather than participants.

And here's the moment something finally snapped in me: I kept waiting for the system to work. Then I realized the system has been working. It just wasn't designed to serve the people. It was designed to keep us fighting, wanting, waiting, and expecting change—while protecting property, process, and power.

Reading this may make you uncomfortable. It may make you angry. It may make you defensive. That's fine. I'm not here to soothe anyone. I'm here to lay out the truth hidden in the laws, systems, processes, and procedures that have endured over time.

If this book does one thing, I want it to do this: force us to stop arguing about the symptoms and finally face the design.

Contents

INTRODUCTION

I did not write this book because I hate America.

I wrote it because I loved the idea of it, and eventually, I could no longer ignore the distance between the promise and the outcome. That distance is not new, and it is not the product of a single election, administration, or political moment. It is older than that. It is foundational. And foundational things rarely correct themselves without examination.

Like many people, I was raised to believe the system was imperfect but fundamentally fair. If something was not working, it must be temporary. If justice was delayed, it was because democracy is complicated. If inequality persisted, it was unfortunate but solvable within the same structure that produced it.

That belief is comforting. But it is also, I have come to believe, incomplete.

What complicates the story of an "imperfect but fair" system is the presence of patterns.

When the same groups benefit repeatedly over decades, across administrations and political parties, it becomes difficult to describe that outcome as a coincidence.

When the same communities consistently absorb instability, crisis, and uneven enforcement, it begins to look less like bad luck. And when structural outcomes remain stable regardless of which leaders promise change, it raises a deeper question about how the system actually operates.

Patterns rarely persist by accident.

When patterns persist across decades, institutions, and political leadership, they begin to reveal something deeper than disagreement. They begin to reveal the design.

This book is not about partisan loyalty. It is not about declaring villains or celebrating heroes. It is not written to defend one political team against another.

Instead, it attempts to look beyond those identities and examine the underlying architecture—the rules, incentives, and institutional arrangements that shape outcomes.

In other words, it is about structure.

If the same outcomes appear again and again despite changes in leadership, the question is not simply whether something failed. The question becomes whether the system is functioning as it was designed.

Those are very different questions, and they lead to very different responses. A malfunctioning system requires repair.

A system operating as designed requires a deeper investigation—one that asks not only what is broken, but what the system was built to protect.

That is the examination this book invites you to undertake.

We will begin with the nation's origin story—the version most Americans were taught and the historical record that complicates it. From there, we will trace how early power structures became embedded in law, culture, economics, and the daily institutions that shape American life.

Along the way, we will look at how the system responds to pressure: who receives rapid protection and who is asked to wait.

We will examine how scarcity is distributed, how public narratives are shaped, how autonomy is regulated, and how reform is absorbed, delayed, or redirected.

Much of this analysis takes place not in dramatic historical moments but in the quieter machinery of governance: budgets, eligibility formulas, procedural requirements, and legal interpretations that determine how policies function in practice.

This book is not primarily about ideology. It is about alignment.

When resources move quickly in some direction and slowly in others, that reveals priorities. When protections expand under sustained pressure and contract once that pressure fades, that reveals something as well. When certain populations repeatedly absorb the costs of instability while others remain largely insulated, the pattern becomes difficult to dismiss.

You do not have to agree with every argument in these pages.

But I invite you to follow the pattern. Read carefully. Notice what repeats. Observe what remains consistent throughout the decades, administrations, and policy domains. If the pattern holds, a difficult conclusion may begin to emerge—not one born from anger, but from observation.

The system may not have failed. It may simply have functioned. And if that is true, the most important question becomes clear: For whom? That is the question we will examine together.

Not with rage—because rage rarely sustains careful analysis.

Not with resignation—because resignation guarantees that nothing changes.

But with clear attention and honest questions.

The invitation is open. The examination begins here.

CHAPTER ONE - THE PROMISE

I grew up hearing that America was an idea—not just a place or a collection of borders, but something powerful enough to draw people across oceans and deserts in pursuit of possibility. I was taught it was founded on freedom, equality, and democracy, and that with enough work and belief, you could become anything here.

That was the promise—simple, persuasive, and incomplete. Like all enduring stories, it left out the cost.

For generations, that promise drew people from every corner of the world—escaping war, poverty, famine, persecution, and hopelessness. America was described as a place where the future could be rewritten, where effort might outweigh circumstance, and where survival could become stability.

I inherited that belief the way most Americans do—not through careful study, but through repetition. It appeared in classrooms, family conversations, national rituals, and in phrases like "land of opportunity" and the "American Dream." These ideas were not presented as arguments, but as truth.

For a long time, I accepted them that way.

But as I've grown older, something has become impossible to ignore: the American Dream has never been only about aspiration. Its simplicity is part of its power— but it has always been about risk, assuming the race is fair without asking who started miles behind.

People did not simply come to America. They survived their way to it.

They crossed oceans under conditions that erased comfort and certainty. They traveled through deserts, boarded overcrowded ships, and made irreversible decisions. Some never made it. Others arrived only to discover that the promise they had been sold did not fully include them.

Freedom existed—but conditionally.

Opportunity existed—but selectively.

Democracy existed—but within carefully drawn limits.

And still, people came. Or stayed. Or sent for their children.

The story teaches people that their lives are within their control. It reassures the nation that its systems are fair. And it reassures those who benefit most that advantages are earned rather than inherited.

The American Dream endured not because it was true, but because people needed it to be. It gave meaning to sacrifice, allowing people to believe that suffering now could lead to safety later—even if they never fully reached the promise.

I speak as someone who benefits from that endurance. My life—my education, my voice, my ability to question this country I live in—did not begin with me. It rests on choices made long before I existed. Some people came willingly. Others were brought by force. Some were told they were equal, only to be treated as expendable. Others were promised citizenship and delivered labor instead.

America was not built by belief alone.

It was built by people.

It was built by bodies, by labor, by survival, and by systems that decided who would benefit from that labor and who would be denied its rewards.

Telling this history honestly means holding two realities at once. The ideals mattered—but so did the violence used to impose them. When we ignore either one, the story becomes easier to live with, but harder to confront.

This is where this book begins.

Not with rejection, but clarity. Belief alone cannot explain a nation. Structure can. And once you begin to look at structure—who it serves, what it protects, and what continues to produce—the story becomes harder to avoid.

The American Dream did not begin as a guarantee. It emerged from people with little security holding on to hope. The distance between promise and reality—between ideals and how they were carried out—is not a side note.

It is the story.

CHAPTER TWO - THE AMERICAN MYTH

The story we tell about America is not just incomplete—it is carefully constructed.

For most people, that story begins with discovery, progress, and the steady expansion of freedom. Repeated often enough, it stops feeling like interpretation and starts functioning like fact. What remains is not confusion.

It is design.

History does not live only in the past. It shapes the present—through laws, institutions, and cultural assumptions built on earlier decisions. The system that became the United States did not begin with abstract ideals. It took form through land seizure, violence, and hierarchy, imposed by force, formalized through law, and later justified as destiny.

Before any European flag was planted, this continent was already inhabited by millions of people living in organized societies. They had systems of governance, trade, agriculture, diplomacy, and spirituality that had developed over thousands of years. This land was not empty. It was managed, defended, and lived on.

Arrival does not equal ownership.

If someone walks into your home, eats your food, sleeps under your roof, and then declares the house theirs because they arrived, we would not call that discovery. We would call it theft. Distance and time do not change that truth.

Christopher Columbus did not stumble onto unclaimed land. He arrived in places where people already lived and immediately claimed those lands for a distant monarchy that had never set foot there.

His voyage was not a humanitarian mission or an act of curiosity. It was a business venture—a financial and political investment backed by the Spanish Crown. Columbus was promised wealth, status, and governance rights in exchange for land, resources, and labor. Profit was the point.

When he reached the Caribbean in 1492, the Taíno people welcomed his ships. Contemporary accounts describe generosity, cooperation, and hospitality. Columbus interpreted this not as humanity, but as opportunity.

In letters to Spain, he described the land as property already taken "for their Highnesses" and the people as suitable labor"—good servants" who could be made to do whatever was asked of them. This was not a misunderstanding. It was a worldview that reduced entire societies to assets.

Before returning to Spain, Columbus left thirty-nine armed men behind at a settlement called La Navidad. They were not diplomats. They were not guests. They were an occupying force placed on land that was not theirs.

Accounts from the period indicate that these men stole from surrounding communities, abducted Taíno women, and used violence and coercion to assert control.

When Columbus returned months later, he found La Navidad destroyed and the men he had left behind dead. This event is often described as a mystery or a "massacre." It was neither.

The Taíno response was not senseless violence. It was defense and survival. A community reacted to abuse, kidnapping, theft, and armed occupation in the way human communities have repeatedly done throughout history—by resisting it.

Their resistance reflected what they were facing, not who they were.

When Columbus returned months later, he did not examine the conduct of the men he had left behind.

Responsibility was assigned outward. The destruction of La Navidad was treated as proof of Taíno hostility, and retaliation followed. What unfolded was not an isolated reaction, but a pattern—one that would repeat across generations: conquest framed as punishment, violence justified as order, and resistance recast as savagery.

This pattern did not end with Columbus. It repeated.

One of the most enduring examples is remembered not as violence, but as harmony.

The story of the "first Thanksgiving" is often told as a moment of unity—a shared meal between European settlers and the Indigenous people who helped them survive. It is presented as cooperation, generosity, and mutual respect. Repeated often enough, it becomes less a story and more a national origin point—evidence that this country began with partnership.

But the reality did not end at the table.

The Wampanoag people, who are commonly associated with that story, were navigating a world already destabilized by disease, displacement, and prior European contact. Alliances were not symbolic gestures of friendship. They were strategic decisions made under pressure, in a landscape that was already shifting.

Peace, where it existed, was temporary.

Within a generation, the balance broke.

As English settlements expanded, so did demands for land, control, and submission. Tensions escalated into open conflict—not because coexistence had failed naturally, but because expansion required it to fail. The same logic that framed arrival as ownership now framed resistance as a threat.

In 1637, during the Pequot War, that logic reached its clearest expression.

At Mystic, English settlers and their Native allies surrounded a Pequot village and set it on fire. As people attempted to escape, they were shot, pushed back into the flames, or killed where they stood. Hundreds were burned alive—men, women, and children.

This was not described as a massacre.

It was described as a victory.

Colonial accounts framed the destruction as necessary, even righteous. The scale of the violence was not hidden—it was justified. The elimination of a people became evidence of order restored.

The Pequot survivors were enslaved, dispersed, or absorbed under conditions that erased their identity. Their name was banned in colonial records. Their existence was not only attacked—it was rewritten.

And still, the earlier story remained.

The image of shared harvest and cooperation endured, while the systems that followed it—displacement, warfare, eradication—were pushed to the margins of memory. A moment of temporary alliance became the foundation of a permanent myth.

This is how narrative works.

It does not require invention. It requires selection.

What is remembered becomes origin. What is omitted becomes irrelevant. Over time, the story feels complete—not because it tells everything, but because it tells enough to be believed. And what is believed does not remain in memory alone. It shapes what comes next.

To legitimize this violence, language shifted. Invasion became settlement. Theft became expansion. Defense became conflict. Once domination is remembered as destiny, the systems built on top of it no longer need to justify themselves.

Violence established the foundation.

Law formalized it.

Institutions preserved it.

Foundations remember. So do the systems built upon them.

CHAPTER THREE - FALSE SAINTS

History did not turn these men into saints.

We did.

We polished their portraits, memorized their words, carved their faces into stone, and taught their names as if admiration were mandatory—long before anyone was encouraged to ask who they were, what they built, and who paid the cost.

We call them Founding Fathers as if the title itself absolves them—as if fatherhood cancels theft, enslavement, sexual violence, and calculated exclusion.

It does not. It never did.

What a title covers, examination uncovers.

This is not about being cynical or edgy. It is about being honest. A country cannot confront its current structure while continuing to worship its architects as though they were above accountability.

The reverence is precisely what makes the examination difficult — because when the founders are sacred, their choices become sacred, and when their choices become sacred, the outcomes become untouchable.

That reverence has consequences.

By the time the American Revolution began, European settlers had already seized vast amounts of land by force. The conflict that followed is often framed as a popular uprising—ordinary people throwing off the chains of tyranny. The reality was more specific.

The Revolutionary War was largely driven and controlled by colonial elites—wealthy landowners, merchants, and lawyers who sought the ability to govern and profit without Crown oversight.

Indigenous nations had no voice in a war fought over their land. Enslaved people had no claim to their own bodies or labor. From the beginning, freedom had boundaries.

When the Constitutional Convention met in Philadelphia in 1787, the men in the room were not ordinary citizens. They were landowners, creditors, and enslavers whose political power and personal wealth were directly tied to property—including human beings.

George Washington enslaved more than three hundred people. Thomas Jefferson enslaved more than six hundred people in his lifetime. James Madison enslaved more than one hundred.

These are not footnotes. They are foundational facts.

These men benefited directly from hierarchy. They built wealth through enslavement and exclusion, and they had no intention of writing a document that would strip them of their own land, labor, or authority.

They spoke the language of liberty. They called themselves revolutionaries and framed their work as enlightened. Then they wrote the rules.

The Constitution begins with a phrase that still defines the nation: We the People. It sounds inclusive. It was not.

At the time it was written, the meaning was already understood. Enslaved people—nearly one-fifth of the population—were classified as property. Women had no political identity. Indigenous nations were excluded entirely, treated as obstacles rather than sovereign people.

Even among white men, participation was often limited by wealth and status.

This was not an oversight. It was the structure.

The Constitution was designed to stabilize power, protect property, and manage instability—not to guarantee equal human rights or achieve democracy. Its compromises preserved slavery, restricted political participation, and insulated authority from popular pressure. The system worked as intended.

The First Patch: Bill of Rights

The Bill of Rights—Amendments I through X—was the first correction.

It was added in 1791, just four years later, because the public recognized that the Constitution did little to protect individual rights. Several states refused to ratify the document without those guarantees, forcing changes before the system was fully established.

In modern terms, the system failed its first test. Even with those changes, the system remained incomplete.

At the time these amendments were added, slavery was still legal. Human beings were still treated as property. Women had no political voice. Indigenous nations were excluded, displaced, and subjected to violence under the protection of the law.

So when these amendments are praised as evidence of democracy and freedom, the more important questions remain: whose freedom, whose rights, and what democracy?

What was protected in practice was not personhood, but process, power, and property. Although the amendments appeared expansive on paper, their application was selective.

The First Amendment protected speech, religion, press, and assembly, yet it never clearly established who could fully exercise those rights without consequence. The Second Amendment addressed militias and defense, while laws ensured that enslaved people could not bear arms and women remained without autonomy or voice. The Third Amendment reflected concerns about quartering soldiers—an issue primarily affecting property-owning men.

The Fourth, Fifth, and Sixth Amendments promised due process and fair trials, protections that were routinely denied to Black Americans, Indigenous peoples, women, and the poor. The Eighth Amendment prohibited cruel and unusual punishment, even as slavery, forced labor, family separation, and the sexual exploitation of enslaved women remained legal. The Ninth and Tenth Amendments are often described as safeguards of liberty, yet in practice, they concentrated power at the state level, allowing discrimination, segregation, and abuse to continue with minimal federal intervention.

Additional amendments followed, but they functioned less as expansions of rights and more as adjustments to preserve stability. The Eleventh Amendment limited citizens' ability to sue states in federal court, strengthening state authority over individual protection, while the Twelfth Amendment clarified the electoral process without expanding participation or addressing exclusion.

What is most revealing, however, is not what was added but what was never included. There was no guarantee of equality, no abolition of slavery, no protection for women, no recognition of Indigenous sovereignty, and no prohibition against discrimination based on race or gender.

That was not a coincidence. It was consistency.

Even with amendments in place, most people remained invisible under the law.

Women could not vote. Black Americans—enslaved or free—had no enforceable rights. Indigenous nations continued to be displaced, erased, and killed under government authority.

The people writing these laws were overwhelmingly wealthy, male, of European or Spanish descent. Everyone else was expected to live under a system they had no voice in creating. That is not democracy. That is management.

Design, Not Failure

We are taught to treat these men and their work as sacred.

Questioning them is framed as disloyal, and criticism is labeled unpatriotic. But no system strengthens itself by refusing to examine its foundation.

This system was never built to include everyone. It was built to determine who mattered. Each expansion of rights did not come from a shift in conscience among those in power, but from pressure applied by those excluded from it.

The Constitution did not fail because it was ignored. It functioned as it was designed to function—preserving property, protecting hierarchy, and allowing inequality to continue under the authority of law.

Amendments followed over time, not as proof of failure, but as evidence that the system could adapt without surrendering control. That pattern matters. Because it explains everything that comes next.

CHAPTER FOUR - FREEDOM WITH CONDITIONS

The first twelve amendments were patches. The fact that they were needed indicates something important: the people who designed this system never intended freedom or equality to apply universally.

They built something else instead—something flexible enough to adapt under pressure, strong enough to endure, and controlled enough to protect itself when challenged.

That is how change has always operated in this country.

America doesn't suddenly develop a conscience or initiate change. Rights expand only when resistance becomes too costly to suppress—when rebellion threatens stability, when injustice becomes politically risky, or when legitimacy begins to crack. Even then, power rarely sacrifices everything. It narrows the scope of change. It limits what's possible. It offers just enough reform to restore order while keeping hierarchy intact.

That pattern matters when examining the Thirteenth Amendment. It emerged from the extraordinary pressure of the Civil War, the organizing efforts of abolitionists over decades, the resistance of enslaved people themselves, and the political calculations of leaders attempting to hold a fractured nation together.

The country did not suddenly develop a conscience. It responded to a crisis—and even in that response, it preserved a mechanism.

In 1865, the United States formally abolished slavery—or at least, that is how the story is usually told. But that version only works if you stop reading at the headline.

Because the amendment that ended slavery also included an exception that reshaped how control would function going forward, the full amendment:

"Neither slavery nor involuntary servitude... shall exist... except as a punishment for crime whereof the party shall have been duly convicted."

That clause is not accidental language.

It is a pivot.

Slavery did not disappear.

It adapted.

Owning human beings outright had become harder to defend morally and politically, but the economic and social order built on exploitation did not vanish with emancipation. Control simply moved through the legal system. Authority shifted from plantations to courtrooms. Labor extraction continued, now enforced through criminalization rather than ownership. The method changed. The outcome did not.

What followed was not delayed or unintentional.

Almost immediately, Southern states enacted laws known as the Black Codes. These laws restricted where newly freed Black Americans could go, limited the work they were allowed to do, and treated unemployment as a crime. Living without steady employment could lead to arrest. Traveling without documentation was punishable. Even minor offenses carried severe penalties.

For people released from slavery without land, money, or institutional protection, these laws created a closed system. Living without sponsorship from an approved employer meant constant risk of arrest. Arrest became the entry point back into forced labor.

Through convict leasing, prisoners were turned over to private businesses—railroads, mines, farms, factories—where they were forced to labor under brutal conditions. States generated revenue. Companies gained cheap labor. Those trapped inside the system had little chance of escape.

This process was not hidden. It was legal.

Slavery did not end. It changed form.

The federal government did not immediately accept this new order. In the aftermath of the Civil War, the United States faced a choice: enforce the legal end of slavery with real protection and participation or leave power in the hands of those who had built their wealth and authority on bondage.

What followed was not reconciliation, but occupation. Reconstruction was an attempt—brief, contested, and uneven—to impose a different reality on the South through federal law, military presence, and political enforcement. For the first time, white supremacist rule was interrupted not by persuasion, but by force.

During Reconstruction, from 1865 to 1877, something genuinely different became possible.

For a brief moment, that interruption held.

Black men voted in large numbers. They held elected office. Public education expanded. Civil rights legislation was enacted, and federal troops were stationed throughout the South to enforce these changes.

For a moment, the idea of a multiracial democracy was not theoretical.

It existed.

But it depended on enforcement—and once that enforcement was withdrawn, so was the progress.

In 1877, federal troops left the South. Almost immediately, the system recalibrated. Power reasserted itself through law, policy, and violence. Voting restrictions spread. Political participation was suppressed. The gains of Reconstruction were systematically dismantled.

The lesson was unmistakable: rights without protection do not survive.

Freedom, once again, proved conditional.

What followed was not confusion.

It was consistency.

Jim Crow laws formalized segregation across housing, education, employment, transportation, and public life. Political influence was stripped away. Economic mobility was restricted. Violence enforced the boundaries where law alone was not sufficient.

And still, Black Americans built.

They built schools, churches, businesses, community institutions, and networks of mutual support—all under conditions designed to limit them. And each time that progress became visible, the response came quickly and decisively.

In Wilmington, North Carolina, in 1898, a legally elected multiracial government was overthrown in a violent coup.

In Tulsa, Oklahoma, in 1921, thirty-five city blocks were burned to the ground. Many people died. Businesses were destroyed. Thousands were left homeless.

These were not random tragedies.

They were reactions.

Progress exposed the distance between the promise and the reality, and the system moved to close that gap—not by fulfilling the promise, but by suppressing the progress.

Over time, the methods evolved again. Open violence became harder to justify publicly, so control moved into policy. Redlining restricted access to credit. Housing covenants enforced segregation. Urban renewal displaced communities under the language of improvement. Policing and courts enforced inequality through rules that appeared neutral while producing predictable outcomes.

The form changed. The function did not.

That pattern continues.

Each time progress presses against the structure, backlash follows. Gains are slowed, redirected, or quietly reversed while responsibility shifts downward. Blame settles on individuals and communities rather than the system that produces the outcomes.

This is why racism cannot be understood as an attitude alone. It is structural.

It has adapted across time—from plantations to prisons, from direct violence to policy, from visible force to systems that appear neutral while maintaining inequality.

The Thirteenth Amendment ended slavery in law.

It did not end the system that required it.

Once that reality becomes clear, the next question is unavoidable:

If slavery could no longer serve as the primary boundary between who mattered and who did not—what replaced it?

America answered that question by rewriting who

counted as "the people."

CHAPTER FIVE - EXPANDING "THE PEOPLE"

The Thirteenth Amendment revealed an uncomfortable truth: freedom in America was never absolute. Even the amendment that abolished slavery preserved a pathway for forced labor through the legal system.

The amendments that followed revealed something else just as important—something the country has been negotiating ever since.

The definition of "The People" was never fixed.

From the beginning, the Constitution spoke in the name of We the People. But in 1787, those words applied to a narrow group—primarily, property-owning white men of European descent. Everyone else lived under a government that did not fully recognize them. They followed its laws, paid its taxes, and helped build its economy, but had little say in how power was exercised.

Over time, that definition began to change. Not all at once, and not because those in power suddenly became generous. Progress in the United States rarely emerged from enlightenment. It emerged from pressure— organizing, protest, political struggle, and sustained challenge from those excluded from the nation's promises.

When enough pressure accumulates, the system adjusts. Rights expand. The circle widens. Each expansion is framed as progress, even as resistance follows and limits are placed around what has been conceded.

This pattern appears—from the end of slavery followed by Black Codes, to voting rights expanded on paper while access was restricted in practice.

Understanding that pattern explains why expansion never meant surrender.

Who Counts: The Fourteenth Amendment

After the Civil War, the country was forced to confront a question it had long avoided: Who counts as an American?

That question persisted not because it was unclear, but because answering it would have shifted power.

In 1868, more than fifty years after the Constitution was written, the Fourteenth Amendment attempted to answer that question by defining citizenship for the first time. Its opening clause declared that all persons born or naturalized in the United States are citizens, overturning the Dred Scott decision, which had denied Black Americans any claim to citizenship.

The amendment also introduced a principle that would shape generations of law: equal protection under the law.

On paper, the promise widened.

In practice, it remained contested.

Citizenship written into law is not the same as citizenship enforced. The language expanded recognition, but the structures already holding power resisted its full application. For many Americans, legal belonging existed long before practical belonging did.

Who Gets a Voice: The Fifteenth Amendment

Two years later, the Fifteenth Amendment addressed another boundary. It declared that the right to vote could not be denied on the basis of race, color, or previous condition of servitude.

For the first time, Black men were legally recognized as voters.

During the Reconstruction period, that recognition transformed political life. Black men voted in large numbers, held office, and influenced the direction of government across the South.

For a brief moment, a multiracial democracy appeared possible.

But it was incomplete—and short-lived.

Southern states quickly worked around the amendment. Poll taxes, literacy tests, and grandfather clauses blocked participation without overtly violating the law. Violence and intimidation made voting dangerous. Enforcement was inconsistent, and protection disappeared. The right existed. Access did not.

Still Missing: The Nineteenth Amendment

While the Fifteenth Amendment expanded voting rights for men regardless of race, women remained excluded from political life.

For decades, activists argued that a democracy denying half its population a voice could not credibly claim to represent the people. Women organized, protested, and demanded recognition—not simply as citizens in name, but as participants in power.

Even as they were excluded, women were repeatedly called upon in moments of national crisis. They worked in factories during wartime. They served as nurses. They sustained families, communities, and economies while men were sent to fight.

They were essential—until they demanded representation.

After generations of pressure, the Nineteenth

Amendment was ratified in 1920. It expanded democratic participation, but like every expansion before it, it came with limits.

The barriers that blocked Black men from voting were also used against Black women.

In many parts of the country, particularly in the South,

Black women faced the same barriers that had long denied Black men access to the ballot. Legal recognition did not guarantee participation. For millions of Americans, meaningful voting rights did not fully exist until the Voting Rights Act of 1965.

Recognizing the Pattern

Taken together, these amendments tell a consistent story.

The United States did not begin as an inclusive democracy. It became one gradually, unevenly, and only under sustained pressure from those it initially excluded. Slavery was abolished. Citizenship was defined. Voting rights expanded across race and, eventually, gender.

Each change widened the promise.

Each change provoked resistance.

The system adjusted—expanding participation just enough to preserve legitimacy while maintaining the structures that concentrated power.

The promise expanded. The structure adapted.

The distance between them remained.

That gap created the next challenge the system needed to solve.

If legal recognition and voting rights could no longer reliably preserve hierarchy, something more durable was required—something capable of shaping how people were valued, ranked, and treated even when the law appeared neutral.

That solution was race—not just as an identity, but as a system that could replace slavery's role.

Understanding how that structure was built—and how it shaped everyday life—is where the story turns next.

CHAPTER SIX -RACE AND SUPREMACY

Race in America was not discovered. It was constructed.

The terms, White, Black, and Brown did not emerge as neutral descriptions of human difference. They developed over time through law, economics, and political strategy. These categories were created not simply to describe human variation—which is real and complex—but to rank it.

Human beings do have physical differences. Those differences developed over thousands of years through geographical climate and genetic variation. But difference alone does not create hierarchy. Hierarchy begins when societies decide what those differences mean—and how power will attach to them.

In colonial America, that meaning was assigned deliberately.

Dividing the Labor

In the early colonial period, labor systems were more fluid than the racial categories that would later define them. Europeans, Africans, and Indigenous people existed within different forms of enforced labor, and in many regions, poor Europeans and enslaved Africans lived and worked in close proximity.

That proximity created a problem for those in power.

Shared conditions sometimes led to shared resistance.

One of the clearest examples was Bacon's Rebellion in

1676, when poor European farmers, indentured servants, and enslaved Africans came together to challenge the ruling elite in Virginia.

The rebellion ultimately failed, but it revealed something dangerous: when people at the bottom recognized their shared exploitation, they could threaten the entire social order.

Colonial elites took note.

What followed was not a moral shift, but a strategic one—an effort not to eliminate inequality, but to reorganize it.

Laws were passed that hardened the distinction between Europeans and Africans. Whiteness became a protected legal status. Blackness became permanent and inheritable.

Children born to enslaved mothers were automatically enslaved, ensuring the system would reproduce itself generation after generation.

At the same time, poor Europeans were offered small, strategic advantages—not wealth or power, but separation. Lighter punishments. Limited access to land. A social position just above enslaved Africans.

This was not equality. It was insulation.

What had once been a shared class struggle was reorganized into a racial hierarchy.

Race was not an accident of history, realization, or fact.

It was a solution to a structural problem.

By dividing people along racial lines, those in power prevented the alliances that had once threatened them—and made inequality more durable than violence alone ever could.

Not Guests. Not Visitors. Americans

The construction of race did not end with hierarchy—it shaped who was allowed to belong.

This is where another lie takes hold—and it needs to be corrected clearly.

Black Americans are not guests in this country. They are not outsiders. They are not temporary participants in someone else's story.

They are Americans.

Most Black Americans are direct descendants of people who were forcibly brought to this land through the transatlantic slave trade. They did not immigrate in search of opportunity. They were brought here to labor and built much of what this country became—economically, politically, and physically.

Under the very system the United States claims to follow, that matters.

The Fourteenth Amendment is explicit: anyone born on American soil is a citizen of the United States. Not conditionally. Not provisionally. Not selectively.

And yet, Black Americans have consistently been treated as if they are less than, that their belonging requires justification—as if their citizenship is negotiable, provisional, or secondary. It is not.

The tension between legal recognition and lived reality is not a misunderstanding. It is part of the design.

A System Reinforced by Law

Once race was written into law, it became self-sustaining. The hierarchy no longer depended on constant, visible violence because inequality had been built into institutions, expectations, and daily life.

Black Americans generated enormous wealth for this country while being systematically excluded from sharing in it. Even after slavery officially ended, many of the policies that built the American middle class were structured in ways that left Black Americans out.

New Deal labor protections excluded agricultural and domestic workers—jobs disproportionately held by Black Americans.

The GI Bill expanded education and homeownership opportunities after World War II, but in practice was often administered in ways that denied those same benefits to Black veterans.

Reconstruction briefly showed what expanded political participation could allow—but it did not address how wealth and opportunity would be controlled afterward.

Housing policy reinforced the pattern. Redlining—backed by federal policy and executed by private banks—marked Black neighborhoods as high risk, cutting off access to mortgages and long-term investment.

The timing mattered.

Homeownership became the primary engine of wealth accumulation in America precisely during the period when Black families were denied access to it. Wealth compounds over time. A home purchased decades ago becomes equity, stability, and inheritance.

When access is denied at the beginning, the consequences do not remain in the past.

They compound forward, causing millions to start off behind society. What began as policy became structure.

When Power Needs No Explanation

By the time race was fully embedded, the system no longer needed constant, visible force to maintain control. It had accomplished something more effective.
It trained people to see hierarchy as normal.

What began as law became habit. What began as enforcement became expectation. Over time, race stopped looking like a system and started looking like reality.

Opportunities did not disappear openly. They were redirected quietly. Neighborhoods formed along invisible lines. Schools reflected those lines. Wealth followed them.

No sign had to explain who belonged where.

People already knew.

That is why the system endured. It shaped perception—who was seen as trustworthy, capable, dangerous, deserving. Once those assumptions took hold, they began to operate independently of law.

Policies could be written in neutral language. Decisions could be framed as individual. Outcomes could appear as coincidental.

But when the same patterns repeat across generations, institutions, and geography, they stop looking random. They begin to look like the design.

CHAPTER SEVEN - DELAY BY DESIGN

Once the Constitution and the early amendments were written, the real work began, because words alone do not govern nations.

Structures do.

The founders didn't just fear kings; they feared the public. What they built was not a system designed to respond quickly to the will of the people. It was a system designed to absorb pressure without surrendering power—to appear functional while producing minimal change.

We are taught to admire this design. We praise checks and balances, celebrate the separation of powers, and are told the structure exists to protect us. But that same structure prevents the government from responding to citizens in a meaningful or timely way. That isn't a glitch. It's the point.

Representation Shrunk on Purpose

The House of Representatives was intended to grow with the population so representation would remain close to the people. For a time, it did.
Then it stopped.

In 1929, Congress passed the Permanent Apportionment Act, locking the House at 435 members. When the U.S. population was just over 92 million, that meant roughly 212,000 people per representative.

Today, with more than 340 million residents, that number has climbed to over 700,000 people per district—and in many cases, far more.

Representation did not expand with the country.

It contracted.

That contraction has consequences. Larger districts increase the distance between ordinary people and their representatives while making access easier for donors, lobbyists, and organized interests.

Distance isn't a side effect. It's a strategy.

Minority Rule Isn't a Bug—It's a Feature

The Senate deepens that distance. Every state receives two senators regardless of population, granting residents of small-populated states the same legislative power as states with tens of millions of people.

As a result, senators representing a minority of the population can block legislation supported by the majority.

This is why legislation with broad national support—on issues such as voting access, gun safety, or healthcare—can stall indefinitely in the Senate despite majority public approval.

This imbalance is not accidental. The Senate was designed to slow change and protect elites from popular pressure.

Add the filibuster—a practice not found in the Constitution but treated as doctrine—and minority rule becomes routine.

This isn't balance. It's paralysis with good manners.

The Supreme Court: Power Without Consent

Then there is the Supreme Court.
Its size—nine justices—is not constitutional; it was set by Congress in 1869. Justices serve for life, shaping law and

policy for generations without elections, accountability, or meaningful removal.

Lifetime appointments were framed as independence. But independence without accountability becomes insulation, and insulation becomes unchecked power. As the country expanded—more people, more states, more institutions— accountability did not expand alongside it.

Power didn't spread.

It entrenched.

Delay Is the Most Effective Form of Denial

Stopping progress outright would be obvious. It would provoke resistance.

Delay is more effective. It exhausts people, drains momentum, and converts moral clarity into procedural confusion. The American system delays so efficiently that stagnation can be framed as responsibility.

Congress spends more time managing process than delivering outcomes. Debates over whether to debate replace action. Hearings substitute for enforcement. Outrage is staged while conditions on the ground remain unchanged.

Committees convene. Investigations are announced. Everything is "under review," "under consideration," or "too complex to rush."

People sense the problem even if they struggle to name it. Americans watch hearings expecting accountability, only to receive performance—witnesses dodge questions, claim memory lapses, or refuse to answer outright.

Even when consequences are demanded, the process slows further. Constitutional protections, political discretion, and interbranch referrals stretch timelines until attention fades. Enforcement becomes inconsistent. Scandals become news cycles. The people affected are left where they started.

This is how oversight becomes delay.

And delay becomes denial.

Urgency is framed as recklessness. Justice is dismissed as impatience. Rules designed to prevent abuse end up protecting inaction. Bills are introduced knowing they will die in committee. Votes are postponed until public attention moves on. Policies with overwhelming support are labeled "too divisive," while legislation that threatens power is buried under amendments until it becomes meaningless.

Nothing is explicitly blocked. It simply never finishes.

Selective Speed

Here is how you know the delay is intentional: the system moves quickly when power demands it.

When banks fail, Congress acts overnight. When markets panic, money appears instantly. When corporations require protection, rules are rewritten without hesitation. Military spending advances rapidly. Foreign aid moves quickly. New wars become urgent necessities, and billions are approved overnight.

So this system is not slow, and America is not broke.

It is selective.

A democracy that cannot respond to the material needs of its people—but responds immediately to the needs of capital—is not unfinished or overwhelmed.

It is constrained. It is captured.

And it is serving exactly who it was designed to serve.

CHAPTER EIGHT -DIVISION BY DESIGN

This is not a metaphor; it is modern American politics.

The United States didn't drift into division. It was steered there. When institutions stopped delivering material improvements for ordinary people, conflict became more useful than solutions. Division didn't break the system.

It stabilized it.

Red versus blue is not democracy in action. It is power reframing politics as spectacle.

Political parties don't appear anywhere in the Constitution. Early American leaders warned about factions because they understood exactly what factions become: loyalty machines that replace public accountability with team discipline.

They were right.

Representation was supposed to move upward:

Citizens → Representatives → Law Today, it often moves sideways:

Parties → Donors → Power → Law

Most elected officials are no longer evaluated by what they deliver to voters. They are evaluated by party obedience, fundraising totals, and media reliability. Step out of line, and access disappears. Money dries up. Your own side will approve of your destruction. Stay loyal, repeat the approved lines, follow the script, and almost any failure becomes forgivable.

That isn't representation.

That's risk management.

Americans are told every election is the most important of our lifetime. Vote harder. Fear more. Donate now.

And yet, decade after decade, the material outcomes remain familiar. Wages barely move. Housing becomes less affordable.

Healthcare remains tied to employment. Student debt expands. Corporate profits reach record highs while ordinary people continue to struggle.

Red wins—the structure holds.

Blue wins—the structure holds.

Because the boundaries never move.

Cultural conflict dominates headlines while economic outcomes remain remarkably consistent.

That isn't a coincidence. It's containment.

Fear and the Convenient Battle

Control doesn't start with laws.
It starts with fear.

Fear of crime. Fear of outsiders. Fear of losing status, faith, identity.

Fear-based messaging increases turnout, donations, and engagement even when threats are exaggerated or false. Fear doesn't need to be accurate. It just needs to be constant.

A scared population doesn't ask structural questions.

It asks who to blame. Or who will make it stop? That's why fear is almost always aimed sideways, never upward.

Managed Consent

Citizens don't vote on many of the decisions that shape everyday life. The federal budget, military spending, corporate subsidies, foreign aid packages, tax loopholes, interest rates, mergers, and other major regulatory frameworks are all determined far from direct public input.

Those decisions are often made quickly when elite interests are involved. Meanwhile, both parties argue loudly while public money is spent with little meaningful public control.

We're allowed to choose the actors.

We're not allowed to change the script.

That isn't democracy. It's managed consent.

This is how democracies decay—not through sudden collapse, but through obedience disguised as participation.

Elections continue. Rituals continue.

Democracy hollows out quietly, not because people stop voting, but because voting stops delivering on its promises.

The Questions We're Trained Not to Ask

A divided public is easier to manage than a unified one. Anger gets aimed sideways instead of upward. Economic pain gets translated into cultural blame.

As long as Americans argue about teams, symbols, and personalities, the most dangerous questions remain unasked:

Why hasn't the House expanded with the population since the early 1900s?

Why hasn't the Senate's structure changed since 1789? Why do a handful of unelected judges get to shape the country for generations?

Why do systems that survive every election rarely change?

A democracy that cannot materially improve the lives of its citizens is not failing.

It is functioning exactly as designed.

But distraction alone cannot sustain a system this durable.

Conflict explains where attention goes. It does not explain why so many people remain constrained even when outcomes never meaningfully change.

For that, something more material is required.

Control is enforced through conditions people are made to live inside — housing, healthcare, wages, and stability that always feel just out of reach.

That pressure does not look like deprivation. It looks like scarcity — selectively applied.

CHAPTER NINE - SELECTIVE SCARCITY

Scarcity in America is not constant.

It is applied.

The country is often described as lacking resources when it comes to supporting ordinary people. It is said there is no money for affordable housing, healthcare, childcare, or wage stability. These are framed as difficult tradeoffs—costly, complicated, and limited.

At the same time, large-scale support for corporations, financial institutions, and markets moves quickly and with far less resistance.

This contrast is not subtle.

It is consistent.

When major institutions face risk, intervention is immediate. When markets destabilize, resources appear. Bailouts are framed as necessary. Subsidies are described as an investment. Tax reductions are positioned as incentives for growth.

The function is support. The language is different.

When assistance moves upward, it is not framed as dependency.

When assistance moves downward, it is framed that way.

That difference shapes perception.

It also shapes policy.

For many Americans, the gap between income and cost of living is not theoretical. It is a daily equation they are forced to solve.

Consider a two-person household earning $42,000 a year—roughly $3,500 a month before taxes and closer to $2,800–$3,000 after. On paper, they sit just above 200% of the federal poverty level, a line that quietly disqualifies them from many forms of assistance. On paper, this is stability.

In reality, it isn't.

The national average rent for a modest two-bedroom apartment ranges from $1,600 to $1,800 a month. Add transportation—$700 for a basic car payment, insurance, and gas. Utilities can add $300. Groceries for two run $600 or more. **Add it up:**

Rent: $1,700
Transportation: $700
Utilities: $300
Food: $600
Total: $3,300 per month

Those totals meet or exceed take-home pay before accounting for healthcare, debt, childcare, or emergencies.

This is the math people live with.

At 205% of the poverty line, this household is technically "above need" while functionally unable to meet basic costs without strain. The system does not measure what life costs. It measures income against a fixed number.

There is little room for savings.

Little room for emergencies.

No room for wealth-building.

This is not mismanagement. It is math.

Public debates about assistance often treat benefits as if they function like income. Critics claim that households receiving aid are effectively earning more than low-wage workers.

That comparison collapses under scrutiny.

Healthcare, food assistance, and childcare subsidies are not cash. They cannot be redirected toward rent, utilities, transportation, or emergencies. Treating them as equivalent to income misrepresents how families actually navigate financial instability.

More importantly, these benefits disappear abruptly.

If a household earns below a threshold, support may be available. If they earn slightly above it—even by a dollar or two—that support can vanish.

The change is not gradual.

It is immediate.

A small raise can trigger increased rent contributions, loss of food assistance, and loss of healthcare—all at once. The value of what is lost often exceeds the added income.

This is not an unintended gap.

It is built into the structure.

People are expected to move forward while the supports that made stability possible are removed beneath them.

Even when assistance is available, accessing or maintaining it is not simple.

Programs are fragmented. Applications are separate. Documentation must be submitted repeatedly. Waiting lists stretch for months or years. Eligibility must be re-proven again and again.

The process assumes consistency from people whose lives are defined by instability.

Time becomes a barrier.

Process becomes a barrier.

Stability becomes conditional.

Help is not absent.

It is difficult to reach.

And once reached, it remains fragile.

Housing policy reveals the deeper design.

The system is often willing to spend thousands of dollars per year subsidizing rent for long periods. Over several years, that support can total amounts large enough to change a family's financial trajectory.

But it is not structured to do so.

Rental subsidies maintain access without creating security. They do not build equity. They do not produce ownership. Payments flow outward while households remain exposed.

The household remains housed.

The system remains unchanged.

Ownership would disrupt that balance.

Subsidy preserves it.

This pattern becomes impossible to ignore.

Citizens pay taxes on income, purchases, housing, and services. Those funds support the same system that later tells them assistance is limited, conditional, and difficult to access.

At the same time, corporations receive support quickly, often without equivalent scrutiny or stigma. Losses are absorbed. Risk is redistributed. Failure is stabilized.

When corporations are assisted, it is described as necessary.

When individuals are assisted, it is described as a burden.

The difference is not financial.

It is structural.

A system that moves quickly to protect capital but slowly to support people is not neutral.

A system that repeatedly subsidizes failure at the top while restricting relief at the bottom is not inconsistent.

It is aligned.

Scarcity is not the absence of resources.

It is the mechanism through which pressure is maintained.

Once that becomes visible, the question changes.

It is no longer a question of whether the system can provide support.

It is who the system is designed to stabilize—and who is expected to endure without it.

Living under sustained pressure changes how people engage with the world.

When survival absorbs energy, attention narrows.

Decisions become immediate. Long-term analysis feels abstract. Participation begins to feel risky rather than empowering.

This does not require ignorance.

 It requires exhaustion.

A population managing constant financial exposure is easier to distract, easier to divide, and harder to organize. Not because people do not care, but because caring costs time, stability, and energy that many lack.

Scarcity does more than restrict options. It reshapes perception.

And that is where control no longer relies only on budgets or policy thresholds. It moves into narratives, language, information, and attention itself.

This is where material pressure becomes something else.

It becomes reality as it is framed, filtered, and fought over.

CHAPTER TEN - WEAPONIZED REALITY

Once scarcity starts to make sense—once you see that resources exist but are distributed unevenly—something shifts.

A harder question emerges: if the system works this way, why doesn't everyone see it clearly?

The system survives not because people are uninformed or unwilling to pay attention, but because it weaponizes what people deem important and patriotic.

Reality itself is shaped, filtered, and redirected until clarity feels out of reach. Control no longer requires silence the way it once did. In many ways, it works more effectively through noise.

There is no shortage of information. In fact, there is so much of it that attention becomes unstable. Each day brings new headlines, new outrage, and new conflicts demanding immediate reaction. Before one issue has time to settle, another replaces it. Before people can process what, they are seeing, the narrative shifts again.

While attention moves, decisions do not stop.

Budgets pass. Policies change. Regulations are written. Courts issue rulings that determine how money flows, who receives protection, and who absorbs risk. These decisions rarely hold public attention for long, even though their consequences last for years. Public focus tends to follow moments, while power operates through systems that continue best whether anyone is watching or not.

Many people sense this disconnect even if they don't always name it. You hear that the economy is strong and institutions are stable, yet rent increases, groceries cost more, insurance premiums climb, and paychecks stretch less each month. You see a crime against the country's capital as an existential threat. Charges are filed. Sentences are handed down. Then time passes. Power shifts. With a change in authority, the same event is reframed—as patriotism, as resistance, a fight to "save democracy."

Official language sounds reassuring, but daily life contradicts it.

That gap—between lived experience and official narrative—is where control becomes most effective.

When people begin to question their own perception, they stop examining structure and start arguing about interpretation. Conversations shift away from outcomes and toward opinions. Reality becomes something to debate rather than something to analyze. In that environment, clarity weakens and confusion settles in.

Language plays a central role in sustaining that confusion. How problems are described determines how they are understood and which solutions feel possible. Workers are not described as underpaid; they are labeled "unskilled." Healthcare is not portrayed as inaccessible; it is framed as "complex." Corporate decisions that suppress wages or cut jobs are framed as "efficiency" or "optimization," while poverty is reframed as personal failure rather than structural design.

Even assistance is framed in ways that quietly shift responsibility. People do not receive support; they qualify for it. They do not have guaranteed rights; they meet criteria. Stability is not something the system ensures; it is something individuals must continually prove they deserve.

Language, in this sense, does not merely describe reality.

It narrows it.

Fear reinforces the same pattern. It remains one of the most reliable tools of control because it captures attention and directs it at the same time. Fear of crime. Fear of outsiders. Fear of cultural change. Fear of losing status, religion or identity.

A population focused on fear rarely looks upward toward systems or institutions. Attention shifts sideways. Frustration becomes misdirected. Structural questions go unasked.

Political conflict intensifies this effect. While political parties represent real differences, the emotional pull of partisan identity often transforms politics into team loyalty rather than public accountability. Criticism begins to feel like betrayal. Alignment becomes more important than evaluation.

Meanwhile, many outcomes remain consistent regardless of which party holds power. Industries maintain influence across administrations. Lobbying, campaign financing, and institutional relationships continue with little disruption. The arguments change.

The structure producing the outcomes does not.

This constant cycle produces exhaustion.

When people are overwhelmed—managing rising costs, long work hours, and persistent instability—they have less time and energy to analyze policy or organize for change.

Survival takes priority.

Exhaustion shifts people from participation to coping. And coping does not challenge systems.

Reality does not require agreement. It exists whether it is acknowledged or not. The constant effort to redefine what is reasonable or acceptable is not evidence of clarity. It is evidence that control depends on interpretation rather than consistency.

When even foundational conversations—about biology, language, or religious expression—become endless arguments, attention is consumed by conflict rather than directed toward structure. When people are pressured to change how they speak, practice their beliefs privately, or adjust their moral compass to avoid conflict, control has already succeeded.

Once you notice how attention is redirected, how language reshapes problems, and how fear redirects blame, the pattern becomes difficult to ignore.

At that point, the question changes.

The issue is no longer which side is right. It is that the structure continues to produce the same outcomes regardless of surface-level conflict.

Because once reality stops being something you are told and becomes something you examine, the system must rely on something more concrete to sustain itself.

And that next layer is impossible to ignore.

It isn't messaging.

It isn't identity.

It isn't narrative.

It's money.

CHAPTER ELEVEN - THE MONEY NEVER LIES

If you want to understand what a country truly values, listen to its speeches.

Then ignore them.

Look at the budget instead.

Budgets are often treated as technical documents reserved for economists and policy specialists. In reality, they are moral documents expressed in numbers. They reveal what a government chooses to protect, what it chooses to fund, and who it expects to absorb the consequences when resources are limited.

Speeches and campaigns can say anything. But budgets show what is actually funded—and what is consistently left out.

Money moves differently than words.

For decades, Americans have been told the same story: there isn't enough money.

Not enough for universal healthcare.

Not enough for affordable housing.

Not enough for childcare, education, infrastructure, or paid family leave.

These programs are framed as unrealistic, financially difficult, or politically impractical. Support for households is often described as a burden—something taxpayers cannot sustain.

Then look at what the budget funds without hesitation.

In fiscal year 2023, U.S. defense spending reached approximately $858 billion—more than the combined military spending of several other major powers. That level of spending has remained stable or increased across both Democratic and Republican administrations. It represents a significant share of discretionary spending and supports a global military presence, advanced weapons systems, and long-term defense contracts.

Debates over this spending rarely carry the same urgency about fiscal restraint that accompanies proposals to expand healthcare or social programs.

The issue is not whether resources exist.

It is how they are prioritized.

A similar pattern appears in tax policy. Federal tax codes include provisions that reduce the amount of revenue collected from corporations and high-income individuals—policies such as accelerated depreciation, preferential treatment of investment income, and industry-specific deductions.

These are often described as technical features of the tax system. In practice, they function like spending decisions. The difference is direction: instead of funds flowing into public programs, resources remain in private hands—disproportionately at the top.

Grace flows upward. Consequences flow down.

Healthcare makes this pattern impossible to ignore.

The United States spends more per person on healthcare than any other high-income nation. Yet millions of people delay care, avoid treatment, or remain uninsured or underinsured. Health outcomes often lag behind countries that spend less and guarantee universal access.

This is not a contradiction. It is a design.

The system is not structured primarily to guarantee care. It is structured to generate revenue through the control of access to care. Money flows through insurance companies, hospital systems, administrative layers, and profit structures before it reaches patients—if it reaches them at all.

Various analyses have suggested that universal coverage models could reduce overall costs by lowering administrative overhead and restructuring incentives. But the current system generates substantial revenue for multiple industries. Those industries invest heavily in lobbying and political influence to maintain the status quo.

These outcomes are not accidental.

They reflect aligned incentives.

The same pattern appears when spending reductions are proposed. Cuts often begin with programs serving populations with the least political influence: food assistance, housing vouchers, public transportation, education funding, and healthcare for low-income households.

Programs benefiting powerful industries or wealthy constituencies are rarely the first targets.

Fiscal responsibility becomes selective.

Assistance for households is framed as unsustainable. Yet similar scrutiny is rarely applied to military spending, tax advantages for high earners, or subsidies directed toward major industries.

The selective use of restraint reveals more than the rhetoric itself.

When budgets are understood as expressions of intent rather than limitations, the conversation about affordability changes.

The United States has one of the largest economies in the world. The constraint is not absolute scarcity—it is allocation.

Looking across multiple administrations and economic cycles reveals a consistent pattern. Financial systems receive rapid support during crises. Corporate continuity is protected. Military funding remains stable or expands.

Programs aimed at stabilizing working-class households are more often debated, delayed, or reduced.

A malfunction would produce random outcomes.

What we observe instead is alignment.

Budgets do not explain everything about a system.

But they rarely lie.

Once you follow the money, power becomes easier to see.

Who benefits from these allocations?

Who absorbs the cost when budgets tighten?

What interests are being protected?

What needs are being deferred—and at what long-term cost?

These questions move beyond party identity and toward the structures that shape policy outcomes.

The central issue has rarely been a single election or political figure. It lies in the institutional architecture that consistently directs resources toward certain priorities while asking others to wait, adapt, or endure.

Learning to read budgets is not an abstract exercise.

It is a practical way to understand how power operates in the society you live in.

And once that pattern becomes visible, a more important question emerges: If the design is clear in the budget— where else does it show up?

CHAPTER TWELVE - THE DESIGN REVEALED

By now, the pattern should feel familiar—not because it is simple, but because it is consistent.

No matter who holds office, ordinary people hear the same explanations and the same limits on what is supposedly possible. Meanwhile, the same institutions remain protected, the same interests remain stable, and the same outcomes repeat.

This is where the pieces lock together.

If the same results appear regardless of political conflict, then the conflict is not the source of the outcome. The design is.

Budgets are not neutral documents. They are instructions written in numbers, showing what must be protected, what can be delayed, and who is expected to absorb risk when resources tighten.

Across time, the priorities remain clear. Funding moves quickly toward financial stability, military capacity, and corporate continuity, while funding for housing, healthcare, wages, education, and long-term public stability encounters resistance and delay.

That difference is not about feasibility. It is about alignment.

When powerful institutions require support, resources appear quickly. When households need support, the conversation slows.

Elections change the cast, but they rarely change the script.

As a result, public life becomes cultural rather than structural. Cultural debates dominate attention while material outcomes remain largely unchanged. Identity replaces incentive. Symbol replaces system.

This system does not rely on force. It operates through vulnerability.

When healthcare is tied to employment, losing a job threatens survival. When housing consumes income, risk narrows choice. When debt compounds, options shrink. Under those conditions, organizing begins to feel dangerous, and stability becomes conditional.

Control works best when it feels normal.

Crises reveal this design most clearly. Decisions are made quickly, and priorities become visible. Markets stabilize. Institutions are protected. Assistance for households follows later—unevenly, conditionally, and through complex processes.

This pattern is not failure. It is function.

Understanding that difference changes the question.

The issue is no longer whether the system works. It does.

The real question is who it works for.

Once that becomes visible, attention shifts. People stop asking what is broken and start asking what is being preserved.

That shift matters, because systems do not reform themselves out of conscience. They respond to pressure, or they harden.

What makes this design durable is not any single policy or institution.

It is the way its components reinforce one another.

Scarcity limits time, energy, and security.

That vulnerability narrows attention.

Narrowed attention makes perception easier to shape.

Shaped perception absorbs conflict and redirects blame.

And while attention is consumed elsewhere, budgets continue to reflect the same priorities.

Each part stabilizes the next.

When financial pressure keeps people focused on survival, participation becomes conditional.

When participation weakens, accountability fades.

When accountability fades, institutions operate with greater insulation.

And when institutions are insulated, their priorities rarely change.

The design does not require public agreement.

It does not require deception at every level.

It requires alignment.

As long as scarcity constrains, narratives distract, and money flows consistently in one direction, outcomes remain stable—even as dissatisfaction grows.

This is why reform gestures can be absorbed without altering the underlying structure.

The system does not resist change directly.

It contains it.

And when underlying structures become visible to enough people, stability no longer looks like fairness.

It looks like exposure.

CHAPTER THIRTEEN - THE STABILITY MYTH

This moment did not appear out of nowhere.

What many people describe as polarization is not new. What is often labeled division is not sudden, and what looks like chaos is rarely accidental. What we are witnessing is not collapse, but exposure.

Exposure.

For generations, Americans were offered a familiar reassurance. If something felt unfair, progress simply took time. If rights were delayed, democracy was messy. If suffering continued, the explanation must lie with the opposing political party. The solution, people were told, was patience—stay engaged, participate again, and vote harder next time.

That narrative works only as long as improvement feels possible.

Over the past several decades, a growing number of Americans have experienced a widening gap between official optimism and daily reality. Housing costs have risen faster than wages in most regions. Healthcare remains one of the leading drivers of personal debt. Inflation steadily erodes purchasing power even when employment numbers appear strong. Younger generations feel less confident about retirement security than their parents did. At the same time, climate-related disasters have grown more frequent and more costly.

As everyday experience drifts further from official assurances, trust begins to erode.

Economic data reflects the strain many households already feel. Adjusted for inflation, real wages for non-supervisory workers have grown only modestly since the late 1970s, even as worker productivity has increased dramatically. The wealth generated by that productivity did not disappear. It accumulated through corporate profits, investment returns, and executive compensation.

The pattern becomes even clearer when looking at who captures economic growth. In 1965, CEOs earned roughly twenty times what a typical worker earned. Today, many earn more than three hundred times as much.

In practical terms, that means companies grew more productive and profitable, but most of the gains went to executives and shareholders — not to the workers who kept those companies running. Wages flattened. Executives' pay exploded.

Housing shows what that imbalance does in daily life. In no U.S. state can a full-time minimum-wage worker afford a modest two-bedroom apartment at fair-market rent. Even people working full-time are increasingly priced out of basic housing, not because they failed, but because wages did not keep pace with costs.

Healthcare follows the same pattern. Costs rise every year, but access remains tied to jobs, paperwork, and the ability to pay. Many people technically "have insurance" yet still avoid doctors because deductibles, co-pays, and surprise bills make care unaffordable.

Student debt completes the picture. Millions were told higher education was the path to stability, then charged for it in ways that follow them for decades. Instead of opening doors, debt often delays homeownership, family stability, and financial security.

These pressures don't appear separately. They reinforce one another. When wages lag, housing becomes unreachable. When housing is unstable, healthcare feels risky. When debt piles up, survival replaces planning.

The result is a widening gap between the story people are told and the reality they are forced to navigate.

Polling reflects this shift. Trust has declined across nearly every major American institution—Congress, the presidency, the Supreme Court, financial institutions, organized religion, and the media. These figures suggest more than frustration.

They signal a crisis of legitimacy.

Yet the most common response has been to encourage greater participation in the very processes that produce the frustration. Citizens are urged to stay engaged and trust institutions that increasingly appear unable—or unwilling—to address the forces shaping daily life.

When leaders call for a return to stability, an obvious question follows: Stability for whom?

Financial markets often recover quickly after shocks. Corporate earnings rebound. Major donors maintain access regardless of administration. The institutional infrastructure surrounding concentrated wealth remains remarkably durable.

Households experience something very different.

Rising costs in rent, insurance, healthcare, childcare, and education shape daily decisions. A medical emergency can impose debt that lasts decades. These realities rarely appear in stock indexes, but they appear vividly in lived experience—delayed family formation, anxiety, declining life expectancy in some communities, and quiet withdrawal from civic life.

Institutions may appear resilient while individuals grow increasingly fragile.

When confidence erodes far enough, people stop asking how policy works and start asking something else: Who will fix this now?

In that moment, complexity begins to look like weakness. Oversight becomes obstruction. Rights can be framed as barriers rather than protections.

History shows this process is gradual, legal, and justified as temporary. Norms erode. Accountability weakens. Power concentrates.

What many describe as collapse may be something else. Clarity.

And clarity changes the relationship between people and power. Once legitimacy erodes, institutions no longer rely on trust. They rely on enforcement, narrative control, or force. That shift is where the real danger begins.

CHAPTER FOURTEEN - WHERE POWER BREAKS

If the system were truly untouchable, it would not work so hard to keep people divided, distracted, and exhausted. The energy devoted to shaping perception—through media narratives, cultural conflict, and procedural delay—reveals something important.

The system recognizes its own vulnerabilities.

Power does not primarily fear anger. Anger can be redirected, absorbed into partisan conflict, or burned out over time.

What power fears is coordination.

When individual frustration becomes collective action, it creates leverage. And leverage is the force that has historically altered systems that once appeared permanent.

This distinction matters, because one of the most persistent myths in modern political culture is that organized resistance is futile—that institutions are too powerful to move. That belief tends to surface most strongly when movements begin gaining traction.

Discouragement is a form of control.

History suggests something different.

Major expansions of rights in the United States did not occur because leaders developed sudden moral clarity. They occurred because sustained organizing made existing conditions costly to maintain. Labor protections, civil rights, women's suffrage, disability rights, and LGBTQ protections all emerged through coordinated pressure.

The early labor movement offers a clear example. At the start of the twentieth century, there was no federal minimum wage, no standard workweek, limited restrictions on child labor, and minimal workplace safety protections. Workers routinely faced long hours under dangerous conditions, and those who attempted to organize risked dismissal, blacklisting, or violence.

What changed was not awareness.

It was leverage.

Workers organized, struck, and disrupted production. Profits fell. Operations stalled. Reform became cheaper than resistance.

The Fair Labor Standards Act of 1938 did not reflect generosity.

It reflected pressure.

The same pattern appears in the Civil Rights Movement. Legislative achievements in the 1960s did not emerge from spontaneous institutional goodwill. They resulted from sustained organizing that combined legal challenges, economic boycotts, public protest, and national exposure of state violence.

The movement understood something fundamental: power responds when the cost of maintaining the status quo becomes greater than the cost of change. Boycotts affected revenue. Protests generated attention. Legal challenges created risk. Pressure was applied across multiple fronts at once.

The results were contested, but they were real.

These examples reveal a consistent pattern.

Institutions respond most quickly when financial stability, institutional legitimacy, or political viability are threatened.

When organizing weakens, pressure fades.

And when pressure fades, outcomes shift.

As labor organizing declined—through policy changes, globalization, and sustained opposition—worker leverage weakened. Wage growth slowed, even as productivity continued to rise.

The relationship is not mysterious.

When leverage decreases, so does bargaining power.

The system does not change simply because suffering exists.

It changes when suffering becomes organized leverage.

Understanding that distinction is not cynical. It is practical. It reflects how institutions have repeatedly responded to pressure.

Leverage exists in more places than people often recognize. Local decisions about policing, zoning, school funding, and public services are frequently made by officials elected with relatively small numbers of votes. Workplace organizing continues to re-emerge across industries, including sectors once considered difficult to unionize. Consumer behavior—through coordinated boycotts or purchasing shifts—can influence corporate decisions more quickly than many legislative processes.

Each of these mechanisms is partial on its own.

Structural change rarely comes from a single action.

It emerges when pressure is applied across multiple arenas at the same time—and sustained long enough to alter incentives.

That is where systems begin to move.

Which leads to an unavoidable conclusion.

Follow the money.

Follow the organizing.

That is where the history of structural change has always been written.

And as attention faded, backlash followed. Gains were narrowed, underfunded, or reinterpreted.

This cycle explains something essential.

Progress alters power. Power resists.

The system is not unresponsive.

It is selectively responsive.

It reacts fastest when stability, legitimacy, or profits are threatened. When pressure weakens, reform slows.

That is why division matters. A distracted public applies less pressure. A tired public sustains less resistance. A fragmented public is easier to manage.

Clarity, not outrage, is the threat.

When people understand where pressure actually works, belief in permanence weakens. What once looked immovable begins to look conditional.

Because it is.

CHAPTER FIFTEEN - AFTER THE ILLUSION BREAKS

There is a moment that comes after anger. It is rarely discussed, because it is uncomfortable to acknowledge. It is not loud or satisfying. It feels closer to grief.

It arrives when familiar explanations stop working—when the idea that the system is simply broken no longer explains what people are experiencing.

Design.

For many people, that realization feels like betrayal. Not just of institutions, but of what they were taught to believe. Of the patience they were told would pay off. Of the idea that participation guarantees a response.

It often comes with a quieter, more dangerous thought: If this is how it works, then nothing matters.

That reaction is understandable.

It is also exactly what the system relies on.

Disillusionment does not end civic life. It marks a threshold. What happens next determines whether people remain manageable or become pressure.

The system does not require belief to continue operating. It requires disengagement.

Most people are not unaware. They are exhausted. They are working, paying bills, navigating instability, and trying to preserve what little security they have inside a system that consumes time, money, and attention—while holding them responsible for outcomes they did not create.

That exhaustion is not accidental.

It limits participation.

But something shifts when blame begins moving upward—away from individuals and toward incentives, institutions, and structure. Once that shift happens, the rituals begin to lose their hold.

Voting matters, but it was never designed to carry the full weight of democracy. Elections rotate leadership. They do not automatically change the underlying architecture.

Democracy is structural.

It depends on representation proportional to the population, accountability that can be enforced, and economic conditions that give people the time and stability to participate. Without those conditions, participation becomes permission rather than power.

This is where disillusionment can either collapse into cynicism—or evolve into clarity.

Cynicism feels protective, but withdrawal does not weaken the system.

It stabilizes it.

Clarity does something different. It connects personal experience to structure. It turns frustration into focus.

Recognition leads to questions. Questions lead to investigation. Investigation, when shared, can lead to coordination.

And coordination, sustained over time, creates pressure.

That is where power becomes vulnerable.

History does not move because awareness exists. It moves when awareness becomes organized.

Understanding that changes the role of the individual within the system. The question is no longer whether the system will correct itself.

It is what happens when enough people understand how it actually works.

Because once the design becomes visible, it cannot be unseen.

And once enough people see it clearly, the illusion does not quietly return.

It breaks.

CHAPTER SIXTEEN - THE COST OF KNOWING

By the time you reach this point, something has already shifted. It is not dramatic. It does not feel like empowerment. It feels quieter than that—like a truth settling into place that no longer allows you to look away.

You can see how power moves, who it protects, and how carefully it has been insulated from those it governs.

That awareness does not make you exceptional.

It makes you responsible.

There is a comfortable illusion that knowing is enough. That once you understand the structure, you have done your part.

You haven't.

Knowledge without response hardens into cynicism. Cynicism creates distance. And distance produces exactly what systems like this require—low pressure and low accountability.

Cynicism feels protective. It offers the illusion that disappointment can be avoided by refusing to care.

But withdrawal does not weaken the system.

It stabilizes it.

A disengaged public applies no pressure at all. In practical terms, that outcome is indistinguishable from compliance.

History shows something different. Systems do not correct themselves out of conscience. They respond to pressure—or they persist.

Major expansions of rights and protections did not emerge automatically. They were forced into existence by people who organized, sustained effort, and made injustice costly to maintain.

That record is not a guarantee.

It is a reminder.

Each generation decides whether to continue that pressure—or release it.

This decision does not require optimism. Optimism is temperament. Some people have it, some do not.

Hope is optional.

Responsibility is not.

You do not need certainty about the outcome to participate in shaping it.

Democracy, when it functions, depends on maintenance. It requires attention that continues after headlines fade, participation that extends beyond ritual, and a willingness to confront structure rather than react to performance.

Without that, democracy hollows out. Voting becomes routine. Rights become conditional. Inequality shifts from something shocking to something explained—and eventually, something defended.

This is not speculation.

It is repetition.

Responsibility begins with attention. Noticing where power concentrates. Recognizing when participation stops producing influence. Refusing to confuse spectacle with structure.

Clarity also becomes practical.

Where does your leverage actually exist?

Often, it is closer than it appears. Influence exists in workplaces, neighborhoods, school boards, city councils, and community organizations. Local decisions shape daily life more directly than national narratives.

What does your local government fund?

Who represents your community—and what decisions have they made?

What processes exist for influencing those decisions?

These questions are not dramatic. They do not trend. But they determine how resources are distributed and who absorbs the cost of those decisions.

Understanding that turns awareness into direction.

The cost of knowing is that ignorance is no longer available as comfort. Once you see the pattern, you cannot unsee it.

But the benefit is just as real.

Clarity replaces confusion. Energy can be directed instead of dissipated. Attention moves toward the places where pressure has historically made a difference.

The system depends on people who believe it is fixed.

It is not fixed.

It is maintained.

And anything that is maintained can be challenged.

Once you understand that, passivity is no longer the default. It becomes a decision.

Participation becomes intentional.

Pressure becomes possible.

That does not guarantee change.

But it removes the illusion that nothing can be done.

At that point, the question is no longer whether the system works.

You already know the answer.

The question is what you are willing to do with what you now understand.

Because systems change only when people decide—not once, but repeatedly—not to cooperate with an illusion.

CONCLUSION -NO MORE ILLUSIONS

If you made it this far, something has shifted.

Maybe it was anger. Maybe it was discomfort. Maybe it was the quiet realization that the story you were handed does not match the pattern you have been living in.

For some people, it feels like grief—grief for the country they believed they were in, for the faith they invested in its institutions, or for the years spent waiting for a correction that never arrived.

That moment matters. Because when an illusion cracks, something new becomes possible.

This book was never about hating America. It was about refusing to protect a lie—the lie that the land was empty, that the founders were beyond criticism, that freedom was always the central design, and that the distance between promise and reality is simply the result of unfortunate accidents inside an otherwise fair system.

The history you've just walked through suggests something different. The country was built strategically. Its institutions reflect specific priorities. And the persistent gap between stated ideals and lived outcomes is not simply the result of mistakes.

It is the system working the way it was built to work.

That realization can be uncomfortable. But discomfort is often the beginning of real engagement. Comfort allows myths to remain unexamined. Discomfort invites scrutiny.

Most Americans were taught to admire this country long before they were taught to question it. We learned slogans before we learned structures. We pledged allegiance before we examined how power actually operates.

That sequence was not accidental.

Love that comes before examination tends to be loyal in ways that love after examination might not be.

But genuine patriotism—the kind that strengthens a democracy—is not blind loyalty. It is demanding. It insists that a country live up to its principles rather than asking citizens to ignore the distance between those principles and reality.

Real patriotism asks difficult questions.

You do not improve a machine by applauding it. You improve it by understanding how it works—by learning which levers move what, by identifying which pressures produce response, and by building cooperation around structural questions instead of the divisions that keep people fighting each other.

Outrage alone is manageable. It flares, circulates through media cycles, and eventually fades.

What institutions struggle to manage is coordination.

They struggle with citizens who read policy instead of reacting only to headlines. They struggle with communities that organize workplaces, attend local meetings, and build durable networks of civic participation. They struggle to sustain engagement long after a viral moment has passed.

That is where leverage exists.

Not in a single election cycle.

Not in a single charismatic leader.

Not in moments of temporary outrage.

Leverage grows from informed people working together long enough to matter.

Changing structures that developed over centuries will not happen overnight. But history shows that organized citizens can move institutions that once appeared immovable.

Responsibility does not require certainty about success. It only requires a decision about participation.

Once you understand how systems operate, the choice becomes simple: remain passive, or contribute—within your capacity—to shaping the conditions around you.

The phrase "We the People" was never meant to be decorative language. At its most honest interpretation, it expresses the idea that legitimate authority ultimately rests with the public itself.

That idea has always been contested. It has been narrowed, diluted, and resisted throughout American history by those whose interests benefited from a smaller definition of "we."

Yet the words remain. And words that remain can still be claimed.

The history of meaningful change in this country is not the story of benevolent leaders acting alone. It is the story of organized citizens applying pressure over time—people who were told that change was impossible, who faced defeat, and who kept going anyway.

Their work expanded rights, protections, and opportunities that later generations inherited.

That history is your inheritance. Not the mythology.

The real record of what determined people have accomplished despite resistance.

The illusion may have broken, but that does not end the story.

It clarifies the work ahead.

Study the structure. Understand the design.

Build coordination with others who see it clearly.

Apply pressure where decisions are actually made— budget hearings, local councils, school boards, workplaces, community organizations, and the many unglamorous places where power quietly operates.

Because once the illusion breaks, the question is no longer what the system claims to be. The question is what people are willing to build next.

And that answer has always belonged to We the People.

Notes And Sources

This book draws on established historical, legal, economic, and political research. Sources are listed by chapter for readers who wish to explore the evidence underlying the arguments presented.

Chapter One — The Promise
Pew Research Center. Public Trust in Government: 1958–2023. Pew Research Center Reports.

Gallup. Confidence in Institutions Survey. 2023.

Acemoglu, Daron, and James A. Robinson. Why Nations Fail: The Origins of Power, Prosperity, and Poverty. New York: Crown Publishing, 2012.

Levitsky, Steven, and Daniel Ziblatt. How Democracies Die. New York: Crown Publishing, 2018.

Chapter Five — Expanding "The People"
U.S. Constitution, Amendment XIV.

U.S. Constitution, Amendment XV.

U.S. Constitution, Amendment XIX.

Foner, Eric. Reconstruction: America's Unfinished Revolution, 1863–1877. New York: Harper & Row, 1988.

Keyssar, Alexander. The Right to Vote: The Contested History of Democracy in the United States. New York: Basic Books, 2009.

Chapter Six — The Invention of Race and Supremacy
Morgan, Edmund S. American Slavery, American Freedom: The Ordeal of Colonial Virginia. New York: W.W. Norton, 1975.

Allen, Theodore W. The Invention of the White Race. London: Verso, 1994.

Rothstein, Richard. The Color of Law: A Forgotten History of How Our Government Segregated America. New York: Liveright Publishing, 2017.

Equal Justice Initiative. Reconstruction in America: Racial Violence After the Civil War.

Chapter Seven — The System Was Built to Stall

Permanent Apportionment Act of 1929. U.S. Congress. U.S. Census Bureau. Historical Population Statistics.

Dahl, Robert A. How Democratic Is the American Constitution? New Haven: Yale University Press, 2001.

Chapter Eight — Red vs. Blue Is the Distraction

Sunstein, Cass R. #Republic: Divided Democracy in the Age of Social Media. Princeton: Princeton University Press, 2017.

Pew Research Center. Social Media and News Consumption Studies.

OpenSecrets. Lobbying and Campaign Finance Database.

Chapter Nine — Selective Scarcity

Chetty, Raj, et al. "The Fading American Dream: Trends in Absolute Income Mobility Since 1940." Science 356, no. 6336 (2017).

Federal Reserve Board. Survey of Consumer Finances. Various years.

Organisation for Economic Co-operation and Development (OECD). Income Inequality and Social Mobility Reports.

National Low Income Housing Coalition. Out of Reach: The High Cost of Housing. Various years.

U.S. Bureau of Labor Statistics. Wage Statistics Databases.

Congressional Budget Office. Income Distribution Reports.

Chapter Ten — Weaponized Reality
(See sources listed under Chapter Eight for media, attention, and political influence research.)

Chapter Eleven — The Money Never Lies
Congressional Budget Office. Federal Spending and Revenue Trends.

Tax Policy Center. Federal Tax Expenditure Reports.

Stockholm International Peace Research Institute (SIPRI). Global Military Expenditure Database.

Chapter Twelve — The Design Revealed
Federal Reserve Board. Distributional Financial Accounts of the United States.

Congressional Budget Office. Federal Budget and Economic Outlook.

U.S. Treasury Department. Federal Spending Reports.

Chapter Thirteen — The Collapse They Keep Calling Stability
Economic Policy Institute. CEO Pay vs. Worker Pay Reports.

Gallup. Confidence in Institutions Survey. 2023.

Chapter Fourteen — Where Power Breaks

Lichtenstein, Nelson. State of the Union: A Century of American Labor. Princeton: Princeton University Press.

Harvard Law School. Labor and Worklife Program Publications.

Chapter Fifteen — After the Illusion Breaks
(Interpretive synthesis drawing on sources listed
throughout the book.)

Chapter Sixteen — The Cost of Knowing
(Interpretive synthesis drawing on sources listed
throughout the book.)

Glossary

Birthright Citizenship–The legal principle that any person born within the territory of the United States is automatically a citizen, as established by the Fourteenth Amendment to the U.S. Constitution.

Checks and Balances – A constitutional system in which the powers of government are divided among branches so that no single branch can dominate or operate without oversight.

Civil Rights – The rights of citizens to political and social freedom and equality, including protections against discrimination based on race, gender, religion, or other characteristics.

Convict Leasing – A post–Civil War system in which incarcerated individuals were leased to private companies for labor, often under brutal and exploitative conditions.

Democracy – A system of government in which political power ultimately rests with the people, typically exercised through voting, representation, and civic participation.

Electoral College – The constitutional system used to elect the President of the United States is through electors assigned to each state, rather than a direct national popular vote.

Endnotes – A collection of citations or explanatory notes placed at the end of a book or document that reference sources mentioned within the text.

Filibuster – A procedural tactic used in the United States Senate to delay or block legislation through extended debate.

Federalism – The division of governing power between a national government and regional governments, such as states.

Institutional Design – The structure and rules that determine how political, legal, and economic systems operate. Institutional design includes the laws, procedures, incentives, and decision–making processes that shape how power is distributed and how policies are created. These structures often influence outcomes regardless of which individuals hold office.

Institutional Power – The influence held by organizations or systems—such as governments, corporations, courts, or financial institutions—that shape rules, policies, and outcomes within a society. Institutional power often operates through established structures and procedures rather than individual decisions.

Lobbying – Efforts by individuals or organizations to influence government policies, legislation, or regulatory decisions.

Mass Incarceration – The substantial increase in the number of people imprisoned in the United States beginning in the late twentieth century, particularly affecting marginalized communities.

Meritocracy – The idea that individuals succeed based primarily on talent, effort, and achievement rather than inherited advantages or structural conditions.

Political Polarization – A condition in which political attitudes and identities become increasingly divided into opposing groups with limited agreement or cooperation. High polarization can make compromise and policy negotiation more difficult within democratic systems.

Propertied Class – A social group defined by the ownership of significant property or assets, such as land, businesses, or investments. Historically, political and economic power in many societies was often limited to members of the propertied class, particularly when voting rights, public office, or legal privileges were tied to property ownership.

Public Policy – The collection of laws, regulations, and government actions designed to address issues affecting society. Public policy determines how resources are allocated, how institutions operate, and how governments respond to economic, social, and political challenges.

Redlining – A discriminatory housing practice in which banks and financial institutions denied loans or insurance to residents of certain neighborhoods, often based on racial composition.

Selective Scarcity – A condition in which resources appear limited, not because they do not exist, but because policies and systems distribute them unevenly.

Structural Inequality – Persistent disparities in wealth, opportunity, or power that result from institutional policies, laws, and economic systems rather than individual actions alone.

Structural Power –The ability of institutions, economic systems, or legal frameworks to shape outcomes and opportunities independently of individual intentions or actions.

Systemic Racism – Patterns of discrimination embedded within institutions, laws, and policies that create and reinforce racial inequality.

Voter Suppression – Practices or policies that intentionally or disproportionately make it more difficult for certain groups of people to vote.

Wealth Gap – The difference in accumulated assets between groups within a society, often discussed in terms of income, property ownership, and inherited wealth.

Working Class – Individuals who earn their living primarily through wages or salaries rather than ownership of businesses or investments.

A NOTE ON RESEARCH

This book draws on publicly available historical documents, legal records, government data, and established academic research. Where possible, analysis is grounded in primary sources—including constitutional texts, public budget documents, and official statistical data—and cross-checked against multiple datasets to ensure consistency. The interpretations and conclusions presented are the author's own, based on patterns observed across these sources.

QUESTIONS THAT REVEAL STRUCTURE

Much of this book has examined how institutions, policies, and economic systems shape opportunities across generations. Understanding those systems requires more than focusing on individual actions or isolated events. It requires asking the right questions about how structures operate.

The following questions can help reveal the deeper logic of any political or economic system.

Who benefits?

Every system distributes advantages. Identifying who consistently benefits from a policy or structure often reveals its underlying priorities.

Who bears the cost?

If a system produces stability or wealth for some groups, it often shifts burdens onto others. Understanding where those burdens fall is essential to understanding the system itself.

What incentives does the system create?

Systems tend to produce the outcomes they reward. If certain behaviors are consistently encouraged, protected, or subsidized, the system is likely designed to sustain them.

What assumptions does the narrative rely on?

Political narratives often simplify complex realities. Examining the assumptions embedded in those narratives can reveal which aspects of the system are being shielded from scrutiny.

What happens if nothing changes?

Looking at long-term trends often provides a clearer understanding of where a system is headed. If current patterns remain unchanged, the future often resembles an extension of the present.

Who has the power to change the system?

Understanding which institutions, actors, or economic forces hold decision-making authority helps clarify where meaningful change is most likely to occur. Learning to ask these questions allows citizens to

move beyond political slogans and begin examining the deeper structures that shape public life.

UNDERSTANDING THE SYSTEM IN PRACTICE

Much of the information needed to examine political and economic systems is already public. Budgets, Legislative records, campaign finance data, and government reports are routinely published, though they are rarely engaged by the public in meaningful ways.

Government budgets reveal priorities more clearly than political rhetoric. Federal spending data is publicly available through official databases, while state and local budgets provide insight into how resources are allocated in daily life.

Legislative voting records allow citizens to see how representatives vote on specific policies, beyond campaign messaging or public statements.

Campaign finance disclosures show who funds political campaigns and which interests maintain consistent access to power.

Local governments—city councils, school boards, and county commissions—make many of the decisions that most directly affect housing, education, policing, and infrastructure. Their agendas, minutes, and budget documents often reveal how power operates at ground level.

Examining these materials does not require insider status. It requires attention. Understanding how systems function in practice begins with following decisions, incentives, and outcomes where they are recorded—not where they are advertised.

DATA APPENDIX

POVERTY VS. COST OF LIVING

The federal poverty line does not reflect actual living costs. Many households fall above eligibility thresholds but below true stability. This gap reflects structural measurement limits rather than economic reality.

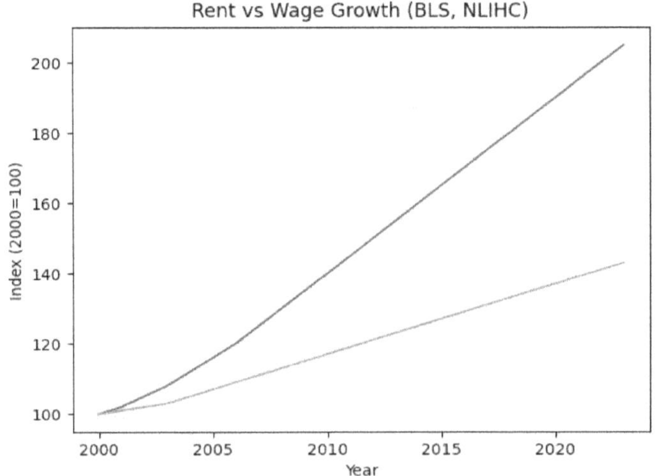

Rent vs Wage Growth (2000–2024). Source: Bureau of Labor Statistics; National Low Income Housing Coalition.

GOVERNMENT SPENDING PRIORITIES

Federal spending patterns reveal consistent prioritization across major categories, including healthcare, defense, and income support.

Allocation reflects structural priorities rather than resource scarcity.

Federal Spending Breakdown. Source: CBO.

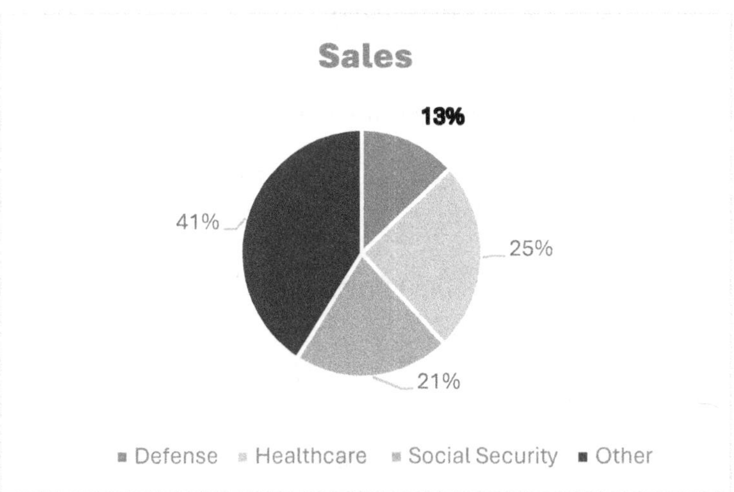

THE OTHER INCLUDES

That "41% other" category in government spending charts is basically a catch-all bucket for everything that doesn't fit into the big headline programs (like Social Security, Medicare, defense, etc.). What's inside it depends a bit on the specific chart or country, but for the U.S. federal budget, it typically includes a mix like:

- **Income security programs**
  (unemployment benefits, food assistance/SNAP, housing assistance, disability support outside Social Security)
- **Veterans' benefits and services**
- **Education, training, and social services**
- **Transportation and infrastructure**
  (highways, public transit, aviation)
- **General government operations**
  (Congress, federal agencies, administration costs)
- **Justice and law enforcement**
  (courts, FBI, prisons)
- **International affairs / foreign aid**
- **Natural resources & environment**
  (national parks, environmental protection)
- **Science, space, and technology**
  (NASA, research funding)
- **Agriculture programs**
- **Interest on smaller liabilities or miscellaneous financial obligations**
  (sometimes interest is separate, sometimes partly included depending on the chart)

The Government has its priorities, and the people have never been among them.

WEALTH AND INCOME DISTRIBUTION

Economic gains are not evenly distributed. Executive compensation has significantly outpaced worker wages over time.

Wealth concentration remains heavily skewed toward the top percentiles of households.

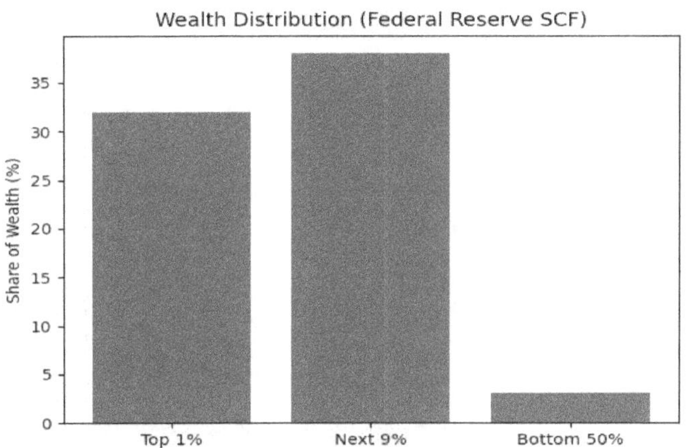

READING THE DATA

The charts presented here are not isolated statistics. They reflect patterns that persist across time, policy, and economic conditions. Individual data points may fluctuate, but the structural relationships remain consistent.

Understanding these patterns requires looking beyond single-year changes and focusing on long-term trends in allocation, access, and outcomes.

SOURCES

U.S. Census Bureau; Bureau of Labor Statistics; Congressional Budget Office; Federal Reserve; Economic Policy Institute; National Low Income Housing Coalition.